First Day of School

Where is my first class?

Today is the first day of school at Sun Valley High School. It is September 7, 2007. Inez, Ron, and Alicia are students at my school. They study their schedules.

I am in English class. My English class is in Room 210.
Our teacher is Mrs. Mendez. She tells us the class rules.

Jorge, Miguel, and Ivan are in the hall. They are in my English class.

Tom is in the school office. It's his first day at our school. The secretary gives Tom a Student Information Form. He fills it out.

Eduardo is in the cafeteria. He eats lunch there every day.

Lily is in the computer lab. Our teacher helps her with the keyboard and mouse.

After school, Victor studies math in the library. He is in the tenth grade.

Questions

A. Do you understand? Write your answers on a piece of paper.

1. When is the first day of school at Sun Valley High School?
2. Who is in the school office?
3. What is the name of the English teacher?
4. Who is in the library?

B. Word Study. Write the word in the correct column.

at   hot   in   is   lab

letter   locker   lunch   math   next

print   Ron   study   ten   sun

Short a	Short e	Short i	Short o	Short u
at				

C. Check Your Work

Compare your answers with your teacher's answers. Correct your mistakes.